Matthew

Shadows soft around his name

A journey through grief

Matthew

Shadows soft around his name

A journey through grief

by

ANN HOLLOWAY

with a Foreword by
The Countess Mountbatten of Burma

BOOK PUBLISHERS

ARTHUR JAMES LIMITED
One Cranbourne Road
London N10 2BT
Great Britain

First published in 1993

British Library Cataloguing-in-Publication Data

Holloway, Ann
Matthew — Shadows soft around his name
I. Title
821.914

ISBN 0-85305-330-8

Cover Design by
The Creative House, Saffron Walden, Essex
and Vicky Tallon

Typeset by
Stumptype, 980-2 High Rd, London N20 0QG

Printed and bound by
The Guernsey Press, Vale, Guernsey, Channel Islands

Contents

The Second Year

Into the Third Year

Foreword

by The Countess Mountbatten of Burma

This memorable collection of poems chronicles the agonising two-year journey of a mother, bereaved of her 18 year old son, through all the emotions and stages of that grief. Stunned anger, disbelief, pain, despair, futility of life, hopelessness, desperate longing and love, slow acceptance — and finally a glimmer of hope and the slow realisation that life still has something good to offer, without ever forgetting the loss sustained.

Sharing this journey with Ann Holloway, who has made it so vivid, is like holding up a mirror to anyone who has been similarly bereaved and can recognise their own heartbreak so truly described. It must also help to explain the nearly unexplainable to anyone who has not suffered that searing experience.

On a practical level, The Compassionate Friends (for bereaved parents) is also deeply grateful for the gift of part of the author's royalties to extend further the help offered by its members to others similarly bereaved.

Although this little book is subtitled *A journey through grief*, Ann Holloway has clearly shown us that we can add two more important words at the end —

"A journey through grief — to hope"

Patricia Mountbatten of Burma
August 1993

Matthew

On June 12th we had telephoned Matthew and Daniel from Malta. All was well.

Returning to our hotel two days later we were given a message to ring home urgently. Fearfully, silently, not daring to speak, we went to our room, and waited with thumping hearts for the call to be put through. Perhaps the house had been burgled? A fire? Maybe the dog was ill? Or the car stolen? Anything, but please not one of the boys.

I'll never forget John's ashen face as he took that fragmented call from his father, the wide-eyed horror, the terrible, trembling quietness before the sobbing, almost incoherent whisper, "Matthew's dead".

There is no way to express the searing impact of those devastating, unbelievable words.

I do not know how we managed the journey home, it all seemed so unreal. At some point shock must have numbed the pain and dammed the tears. We were in a state of stunned disbelief.

Matthew was returning home from his girl-friend's house on an unlit country road which had just been re-surfaced when, for some unknown reason, his car went out of control, hitting a tree and ending up in a ditch. He was taken by ambulance to hospital where, after a brief time in Intensive Care, his condition deteriorated drastically. As Daniel arrived with Theresa, Matthew was being rushed to the operating theatre. He died a little while later after a massive haemorrhage resulting from crush injuries to his chest.

In a few short hours, a life that held so much promise, was no more. John and I had lost our beautiful, precious youngest son; Daniel, in his own words, had lost "not only a great brother, but a great mate as well".

Someone once said "God is too wise to make a mistake, and too loving to be cruel". I hope so.

Why? We asked ourselves and each other that unanswerable question often enough. I don't believe, now, that knowing why could in any way lessen our grief or our longing because I'm sure it would be beyond our understanding. And yet . . .

Although still struggling, as a family, to come to terms with Matthew's tragic and untimely passing, we are gradually re-building our lives, each of us learning to cope in our own particular way. Daniel and Theresa have their own home, not far away, and we — against all odds — are slowly beginning to find some pleasure once more in the activities and hobbies we previously enjoyed. These are things we would never have thought possible.

Matthew is, and always will be, very much part of our lives. We love him and miss him terribly, but for his sake we really do try "to turn again to life, and smile".

The First Year

*D*eath has leapt upon life
And the shriek of the encounter
Echoes on and on through silence
for ever

Part of *Monte Cassino 1945* by Marion Coleman

The church was packed, overflowing,
Grief immense, clearly showing.
For gentle Matt, in his coffin, dead,
Hymns were sung and prayers were said,
then our beautiful son was laid in his grave
And part of me wanted to scream, to rage,
"How can it be, how can it be true,
To have loved and lost, one as special as you?"

June 1990

Why us God?
Why has this happened to us?
What have we done?

And what about Matthew?
He did nothing to deserve this.
You know all your children
so you must have known him
to be a nice lad,
a lad with so many special qualities.

So much potential,
so much goodness, gone.

Gone where? Why?
Gone physically God,
please only physically.
'Only' physically —
It's the physical presence we want.
It's the physical presence
we can't replace.

I don't believe 'he' is no more.
I feel him close to me.
I sense him, smell him, but
I want to touch him, see him, hear him.

I know you are not a cruel God.
Why can't you explain?
Why don't you answer me?
He struggled so hard to be born,
yet he left us so quickly. Why?
What does it all mean?
I don't think I'm angry with you.
Please help me understand.
There are so many evil people,
why are they still here?

Why did I spend the day of the accident
in tears, long before we heard the awful news?
Were you warning me?
Why, O why did he have to go?
And why then, when we were away?
Why couldn't you at least have allowed us
to be with him?

Has he really returned 'home',
his spirit free?
Please God, look after him for me.

June 1990

Daniel and Theresa weep
and Daniel speaks
with cracked emotion,
words from a splintered heart.

Theresa supports him,
supports us,
tiny girl, full of quiet strength,
carrying sorrow
with dignity.

The finality of Death,
this terrible cruel untimely Death,
has forced itself upon them
with such brutality,
that I fear the horror
will haunt them for evermore.

Policemen at the door.
Intensive care.
Too late.
Brother, friend,
Dead.

Screaming, crying, anger, grief,
devastation, terror, disbelief.

Young minds shocked,
turned inside out,
by life turned upside down.

Together we drown.

June 1990

June's bright and scented blooms
   Cover Matthew's grassy bed.
   A blanket of sorrow,
Warmed by sun,
Refreshed by rain.
Flowers of beauty,
Expressions of pain.

July 1990

The evening sun
   cast shades of melancholy over the headstones,
   as we tended the profusion of flowers
on your grave.
No words were spoken.
In silent agreement we sat on the grass,
despair consuming our thoughts,
disbelief arguing with reality.
In unison
our gulping, uncontrollable sobs filled the silence,
as shredded emotions found release
in a torrent of tears.
The dog,
sitting between us with patient understanding,
pricked her ears and cocked her head.
Some-one coming?
The gate creaked open and then closed.
A sensitive person, witness to our utter desolation,
respectfully did not intrude;
leaving us, until, tears exhausted,
we returned to the sadness of home.

July 1990

Your bed remains unslept in,
        Your possessions are all around, forlorn;
        Tapes, after-shave, college work,
Clothes for the office, hardly worn.
In the hallway, Candy, restless with tuned-in ears
Listens for your tread upon the stairs,
I gaze into her eyes and see reflected tears.

July 1990

You've gone Matthew.
        Gone. I cannot understand.
        Gone, left, departed, passed on.
They are only words.
What do they mean?
There does not seem to be an
Adequate acceptable word.
None of this is acceptable.
It's all too unbelievable.
I just can't believe.
Comprehension is beyond me.
You were warm and alive
When we left for our holiday;
Brimming with excitement
When we spoke on the 'phone.
You were going to pick us up
From the station.
But you didn't. You couldn't
Because you had already 'gone'.

You were cold when I stroked your cheek.
Oh Matt, you hated being cold.
You must hate being 'gone'.
I can't say the other word.
Did you suffer?
I can't bear to think about it.
Are you confused? Angry? Sad?
You must be, you loved life so.
You had so many plans.
Everything
Was falling into place for you.
You were so happy
We were so proud of you.
We love you so.
Why did the bubble have to burst?

Are you safe? I'm so worried.
You weren't christened.
Please forgive me.
Where are you Matt?
I wish I could be with you,
To comfort you.
I would have gladly 'gone' for you.
I never knew there could be so much anguish,
So much sorrow, so much pain, so much despair.
I can't believe you're gone,
Just can't believe you're gone.

Goodnight, my son.
May God bless you and protect you
As you journey on.   July 1990

Soft eyes still mirror
    the sadness of her aching heart.
    Soft eyes still spill
her grief, young love torn apart.

Trembling words still cry out
in utter disbelief.
Trembling words recall
a love so good, so brief.

Love that shares our love,
Love that shares our sorrow,
Love that wonders Why?
And fears each new tomorrow.

Donna, you're so young
to cope with all this strain,
to cope with such a tragedy,
to suffer so much pain.

July 1990

I was worried.
    You were late.
    I was on the 'phone,
a nurse explaining,
she'd tried to call us
but now you were on your way home.

22

I heard your bike on the gravel,
not your car.
You walked through the door,
wrapped up against the cold.
I wore a summer dress.

You were younger, hair longer.
I gathered you in my arms
sobbing with relief, asking
"What happened?"

"I couldn't breathe," you replied,
"but I'm fine now. Don't worry, mum."
You raised your head and gazed at me,
deep blue eyes shining
with something I couldn't quite grasp.

I buried my face in your silky blond hair,
breathing in the smell of you.
You melted in my arms,
soaking into me
and you were gone.

I awoke, face wet,
silently screaming
with the torture
of hope torn away.

You said you were fine.
Are you sending me a message?
Can you speak to me in dreams?

July 1990

A potential leader*
     it was so like him to go before us
     into the mapless region of death
thereby diminishing the terror for us.
For however we may recoil
from the invisible torrent,
we shall not be entirely fearful to follow on
into the unfathomable canyon where he has gone.

Part of *20th Century Requiem*,
by Patricia M Saunders

*The original line reads *'Our unquestioned leader'*

My son, how I feel for you,
     For the terrible torment you've been through.
     I feel your sadness and your disbelief
For your brother's life, which was all too brief.

You appear so brave as you carry on,
Though your burden is heavy
You strive to be strong
But I'm aware of the times you silently weep
When sorrow through the armour seeps;
And the camouflage of your sun-tanned skin
Cannot hide from me all the grief within,
For I know your courageous smile belies
The pain so apparent in your eyes.

My son, how I wish I could take away your pain.

August, 1990

I sit in your room.
  Your room is spotless.
  "Finished decorating my room,"
You said on the 'phone. "Looks great."
It does.
Built-in desk and stereo unit complete,
Walls and paintwork gleaming.
O Matt, all your hard work . . . . .

Your room is silent.
Silence closes in on me.
Suffocating me.
I want to scream,
To pierce the silence,
But I don't.

Your room is tidy.
Tidiness is unnatural here.
Here should be a real mess.
I want to scatter things,
Crumple the duvet,
But I don't.

Your room calls out for you.
I call out for you.
Your room is waiting for you.
I am waiting for you.
I can't believe you'll never again return.
O God. Never again return.

August, 1990

25

When I picture Matthew,
So young and healthy,
So full of life and promise,
How can I truly think him dead?
Or that he's really gone forever
With farewells left unsaid?

August 1990

Car enters drive and slowly, so very slowly,
You come indoors.
I'm aware you dread the moment,
Coming home is so painful;
The house may be full, yet emptiness overwhelms.

"What sort of day have you had?"
I ask with a lump in my throat.
No reply. No need for words,
Your eyes say it all as they speak in tears.

What a strain to have to work,
To try to hide the torment and sorrow within,
To see cars like Matt's on the road
And for an instant believe him there.

You sit in the garden, a sad, sad man;
Dog's head resting in sympathy on your lap.
I join you, we talk
But neither can mend the other's brokenness.

I can't remember exactly when
But one day after the accident, you picked flowers
And turned Matthew's bedroom into a scented garden;
Sweet Peas and Carnations everywhere,
Filling the room with your love.

You need some solitude.
From indoors I watch through the window
As you look around the garden,
Knowing you see the past, not the present,
That you listen in hope for the sound of the silent voice
And not to the songs of the birds.

My heart, in sympathetic unison with yours,
breaks a little more.

August 1990

Loving, caring grandparents,
    you have lost your youngest grandson
    and through your terrible agony
you have to watch, in despair,
your own son and his family suffer.

A devastating blow, what will it do to you?
You show courage without
but I feel dread at the tearing within.

You seem so vulnerable.
You age before my eyes,
sorrow, reducing you in size.
Such a price to pay for loving.

August, 1990

Granny was diagnosed as having cancer shortly after I wrote this.

Sorrow occupies my every moment
Denying me oblivion in sleep.
It blinds my eyes, deafens my ears
And confuses my thoughts,
Stealing my concentration.

Sapping what little energy I have,
It clings to me relentlessly,
Binding itself to me,
Seeping into every nerve,
Weaving through every emotion,
Every action,
Halting my movements,
Interrupting my speech.

Brutal in its intensity
It permeates my senses,
Indescribable pain,
Which nothing can relieve.   August 1990

I found him in the garage,
Etching Matthew's name
On the cross he'd made.

Tears coursing down his cheeks,
Grief soaking into the wood,
Sorrow soaking into his face.

And even now, disbelief.
No Dad expects to carve a cross
For his son's grave.   August 1990

I am terrified
   that my mind may be irretrievably lost.
   During the day I crawl back into bed
pulling the duvet over my head,
trying to still my dark imaginings,
convinced I am going mad.
But, try as I may, I cannot control my thoughts
and ever-present longing claims them in victory.

I do not have enough faith in my courage
to endure endless days, let alone endless years without
      you.
If this really is the rest of my life, do I want it?
The alternative is tempting,
but my conscience whispers "selfish".
The family I love has suffered enough.
Yet how can I without dread, look to the future
when all I see is a black abyss?

I am so confused.
I so desperately want to be with you
but it would mean leaving those I love here, behind.
Is this where I'll always be now?
In a kind of purgatory,
torn between two worlds?
An alien in this one
Yet forbidden access to yours.

August 1990

I dreaded I'd have nightmares of you
   imprisoned in your coffin,
   you who loved your freedom.
Often dark thoughts do invade my mind,
without provocation,
to be urgently dismissed
with the worms
and the unimagined decaying body,
the beautiful body,
cared for so well.

But I haven't had such nightmares,
for an inner knowledge,
always urging me to understand
you are not there,
has not allowed such buried terrors
to invade my restless dreams.

August 1990

The cross his Dad so lovingly made,
   Stands at the head of Matthew's grave,
   Where flowers in remembrance still are laid.

August 1990

30

"Sadly Missed, A Brother, A Friend",
Inscribed on a vase of stone.
How my heart aches for the loss Daniel feels,
For together, so closely, they'd grown.

August 1990

There must be a reason 'Why?'
But no answer can I find.
Why an end to your lovely young life?
Why the loss of your gentle young mind?

Only silence answers my questions,
So I must live with the sorrow and pain
And trust in God and believe in my heart
That we shall meet again.

September 1990

W e sat in the living room,
Dad, Daniel, Theresa and I,
the four of us together
yet alone with our own
private thoughts,
each aware of the empty settee.

The sound of a key in the lock
stirred us,
nervously we looked at each other
with searching disbelief,
not daring to voice our hopes.

We waited,
eyes fixed on the door
and there you were,
large as life,
grinning, as you kicked off your shoes
before sprawling, relaxed, on the settee.

Then we were all together,
holding you, touching you,
crying, laughing,
nightmare ended.
"Oh Matt, you're OK." I said.

Time stood still.
Candy, who had appeared from nowhere,
began to whine, then bark excitedly,

barging through us to get to you.
Dear old Shan was with her.
We all accepted this.

We were locked together,
savouring this moment.
No-one wanted to let go.
It was you who moved first,
gently easing yourself free
and reluctantly we moved back.

You stood apart, strong and whole
and ethereal.
You looked at each of us in turn,
smiling a smile that made us cry.
"I'm fine, just fine, don't worry,"
you whispered,
as you slowly faded away.

Tears woke me.
Quickly, desperately, I closed my eyes
trying to recall you
but you had gone
to another place, another time.

Ethereal, I remember using that word
about you when you were a baby.

September 1990

Images of Matthew go around in my head,
Images of Matthew in Liverpool red.
Images of Matthew, proud at the wheel,
Images of Matthew brimming with zeal.

Images of Matthew through all of his years,
Images of Matthew, much laughter, few tears.
Images of Matthew in sunshine and shower,
Images of Matthew, hand clutching flower.

Images of Matthew — they go on and on
Images of Matthew, handsome and strong.
Images of Matthew, fun with his friends.
Images of Matthew, disbelief never ends.

Images of Matthew, so much to fulfil.
Images of Matthew, now silent and still.
Images of Matthew, so alive but now dead.
Images of Matthew go around in my head.

September 1990

Some time after writing this, I read an almost identical poem in *Helping each other through the seasons of grief*, published by The Compassionate Friends

Silently,
on the wings of love you come to me
and I feel your presence near.

Gently,
a perfume fills the air,
this you bring, to prove that you are here.

Softly,
I sense your hand upon my arm, to reassure
"I'm safe, protected from all harm".

Fleeting moments,
then you are gone,
but the memory of our reunion
gives me the strength to carry on.

September 1990

I thought I'd be alright on my own,
   When first I walked through the town alone.
   I thought I could cope, I tried to be calm
But the whole of my being screamed in alarm
For it had not been long since you walked this way,
With eager steps on pavements grey.

And my heart cried out, "Dear God,
Do my feet tread where Matt's once trod?"

The thought struck terror from head to toe.
Fear engulfed me. Where could I go
To escape the crushing, vice-like claw
Of the panic that seized me yet once more?

Blindly I groped through the misty crowd,
Only feet I saw, my head was bowed
As breathless I stumbled into a store,
Heart wildly pounding; emotions raw.

But there was no escape, no relief,
Just agony and disbelief
As music fuelled my hungry grief
Mocking false bravery, which now had gone,
Wrenched from me by Elton John
Singing a song you really liked,
A song you'd listened to that night
When love was young and life was right,
Just hours before your soul took flight.

'It's No Sacrifice' pierced my ears,
While eyes surrendered up their tears
Lamenting your lost earthly years.

September 1990

36

Where are you Matthew?
The 'real' you, not the shell?
Where is the sunshine of your personality
and the warmth you brought to our lives?
Where is your gentleness, your thoughtfulness
and your lively enquiring mind?
Where is your humour and your smile?
A smile which could light the dullest day.

Have you taken with you
All your own unique qualities?
The vibrance of your youth?
The adventure?
The splendour?
The excitement?
I'm sure you have.

Do you feel our love around you?
I'm sure you do.
For wherever you are,
So part of us is too.   September 1990

Absent-mindedly looking into a shop window,
I became aware of a wizened, haggard face.
Parched eyes held my gaze with a fixed stare.
I froze in horror.
Panic gripped me
as I realised I was seeing a reflection
of my tormented self
and the soulless eyes, devoid of light,
were mine.

                                          October 1990

O Matt, no celebrations,
No joyous expectations
Of seeing you today.

No 'Happy Birthday' cheer,
To celebrate your nineteenth year.
No 'Best Wishes' for your future . . .

No card, no presents, no kiss,
No smile from the face I dearly miss
And will for evermore.

I leave my flowers in disbelief,
Senses numb, frozen in grief.
I know that hearts do break.

And Mother Nature cries for you,
Her tears upon your grave as dew,
Sadly mingling with mine.

I cry for you, I cry for me,
For all the things that will not be,
For life's unfinished symphony.

8th October 1990
Matthew's 19th birthday

Today, your birthday,
I prayed for a sign,
a sign to assure me
that you are safe and well
and gathered in the fold.
But whilst pleading for a sign, I was seeking a miracle;
like you'd appear before me
assuring me yourself;
or that your Azalea would flower
now, in October.

The day slowly passed
in frantic searching.
Nothing happened.
I was desperate, distraught
and depressed
Time was running out.

Late afternoon, doorbell rang,
Bridget with flowers
saying she couldn't stay long,
Samantha had dancing lessons.
"What time is it?" she asked.
"Twenty to five," I replied.

We shared tears and chatted awhile,
then she left,
leaving her kindness behind.
She'd planned to come in the evening
but something urged her to come then.   *(continues)*

I closed the door
and sat on the stairs
heavy with sadness.
It was then it hit me.
I caught my breath as an image
of a tiny hospital
identity bracelet
floated across my mind.
'Your miracle, your miracle,'
a voice seemed to say.

I shot upstairs and with trembling hands
picked up 'my sign'.
There it was

BABY HOLLOWAY — TIME OF BIRTH 16.40.

16.40 — Twenty to five.
The exact time Bridget had arrived with her flowers.

This was a real sign, solid evidence,
a prayer answered; a heaven-sent miracle
so real in its simplicity.
Would I have believed a 'big' miracle?
Or would I, later on, have thought it
a figment of my imagination?

I cried with relief and gratitude,
You are safe. I thanked God.

8th October, 1990

I don't belong here any more.
   I feel so threatened away from home,
   away from the village.
Nothing is the same.
Has the town really changed so much
since you left?
There's no space,
it's swallowed up by garish shops,
endless traffic and aggressive people,
insensitive to my grief.

I feel like an explorer
in a strange and foreign land.
A land of disharmony,
where thumping music, harsh sounds
and four-letter words invade my ears.
My vulnerable senses seem under attack.

Has there always been so much graffiti
and rubbish and winos and yobs?
Why did you have to go
when the streets seem littered
with misfits?
Am I seeing life as it really is,
or just tuning in to the dark side?
Is it my own anger reflecting back at me?
I don't want to become bitter.

(continues)

I've forgotten how to function
in ordinary, everyday situations
because nothing is ordinary any more.
I'm not ordinary any more, I'm different.
The fault is with me.

Perhaps I should let people know I'm different,
that I'm a mourning mother.

Perhaps I should wear black from head to toe
and then people would step aside for me
and speak in gentle voices.

Perhaps fraught mothers would find patience
with their children
if they really understood
they are only on loan
and can be called back without warning,
as you were.

Will life and people and places
ever be as they were? Will I?

October 1990

I am daydreaming,
    gazing at the stream in the woods
    after a rainy day,
the same stream where two brothers used to play;
But that was way back yesterday,
in a yesterday now gone.

I picture two blond boys
in coloured wellies;
splashing, laughing, building dams,
racing twigs.
But now I have a price to pay,
for the happiness of yesterday,
for the yesterdays now gone.

O how I long for yesterday
for all the yesterdays now gone,
yesterday I had two sons,
today I have only one.

October 1990

43

I gazed in rapture at Monet's paintings, eyes all
        seeing.
   I felt such emotion, such tearful joy at their sight.
Vibrant gentleness, unreal reality,
The beauty, the colour, the freshness, the light.

His spirit, his personality, communed through the paint,
Stirring my senses, touching my soul
With shimmering mistiness and sunlit radiance.
Wondrous canvasses, so alive, so free,
Awakened so many feelings in me,
Feelings I felt that you could see.

October 1990

I am obsessed
   With Death
   And its shroud of mystery.

"Seek and ye shall find"
Exorcise it from my mind,
Will God really be that kind?

What is human destiny?
And the meaning of eternity?
Do we all gain immortality?

I'll delve and delve unceasingly,
Until I find what's right for me.
Is Death re-birth, not tragedy?

November 1990

Could I have dreamed of being awake
and having a vision of you?
No.
Even though it was brief
it was real,
you were real.

Grey light was replacing darkness.
I know my eyes were open,
I can remember closing them . . .
afterwards
and re-opening them,
to what I then considered
the cruelty of deception,
but which I now recognise
as a blessing, a gift.

I recall rousing to wakefulness
hearing you softly whisper "Mum,"
as you did when you crept in late at night
wanting to tell me something.
I opened my eyes and there you were.
"I'm home, Mum, I'm safe," you whispered.
"Really, I'm fine, don't worry."
Relief and belief flooded through me.
You were you,
I could smell your aftershave.

(continues)

45

I closed my eyes,
glad you were home.
I settled to sleep
but something was wrong.
Eyes quickly opened in panic
resting on the flowers beside your photo.
I heard myself whimper,
felt my heart tear with each racing beat.
O God, such a cruel dream.

Dream, this was no dream.
I closed my eyes once more
picturing the 'vision' I had seen,
the vitality of you,
and peace I had felt around you
and the truth that shone from you.
You are 'home'
and you know more than I,
your eyes told me so.

November 1990

My faith is not blind,
　　Although sometimes I still wear blinkers.
　　I know there is another dimension beyond my
　　　　sight;
Just as I know
That all things visible by light of day,
Are still there,
Though hidden by the dark of night.
With earthly eyes,
Unable to perceive the whole,
The knowledge
Springs, from deep within my soul.

November 1990

*M*atthew will not grow old
　　As we who are left grow old.
　　Age will not weary him
Nor the years his beauty dim.
Each day of each year,
Until our last sunset
We will remember him.

December 1990

An adaptation of Lawrence Binyon's poem, *For the Fallen*.

A Christmas wreath I made for you,
Fashioned with love, it was all I could do.

Holly leaves green and bright,
Christmas roses, snowy white,
Berries shining brilliant red
Confusion racing round my head,
O Matt, I can't believe you're dead
And festive days approach with dread.

Gift complete, respite from tears,
As mind recalling other years,
Gently slips back to a time
When life had reason, life had rhyme
And sobs escape, for I can see
So clearly in my memory,
Those happy times that used to be;
Excitement round the Christmas tree;
When we were four instead of three
And I could hold you close to me.

December 1990

There are times when I am numb
cut off from reality,
cut off from feelings.
This numb is a contradiction
of itself.
This numb is not without sensation,
it hurts.

Unseen tears fall inward,
each one freezing on the previous one
building an iceberg,
which crushes from within.

I am my jailor and my prisoner
shunning, yet longing for release.
With trepidation
I await the welcome threat
of an invading thaw.

Time passes in bleakness
until tortured emotions brave escape.
With relief
I drop my head in my hands,
fingers acting as a sluice
for the ensuing flow
of melting tears.

Heaven-sent remedy, healing balm,
my heart would turn to ice
without them.

January 1991

Who will believe?
the sadness of death,
the terror, the fear, and the emptiness?
What can they know
Of the vacant eyes
The sorrow too deep
In the heart that dies?

Part of *Bomb Incident*
by Barbara Catherine Edwards

God's Lent Child

I'll lend you for a little time
a child of mine, God said;
For you to love the while he lives
and mourn for when he's dead.

It may be six or seven weeks
or thirty years or three,
But will you, till I call him back,
Take good care of him for me?

He'll bring his charm to gladden you
and should his stay be brief,
You'll have his lovely memories
as solace for your grief.

I cannot promise he will stay
since all from earth return,
But there are lessons taught down there,
I want this child to learn.

I looked the wide world over
in my search for teachers true,
And from the throngs who crowd life's way,
I have chosen you.

Now will you give him all your love
and not think the labour vain;
Nor hate me when I come around
to take him back again?

Anon

Dear God, we do not hate you
but we cannot understand:
he had so much to offer —
What is it that you've planned?

Why did you have to take him?
Why then, in such a way?
He brought us so much happiness,
we wanted him to stay.

We're sorry we can't say the words
"Dear Lord, Thy will be done,"
for we love him so and miss him,
he was a fine and gentle son.

January 1991

I am two,
   Can that be?
   I question which one's really me.
One is smiling? Coping well?
The other weeps in a living hell.

One is
Too tired to deceive,
And wants to be alone to grieve.
The other
Tries to battle on,
Even though all meaning's gone.

Some days, one
Is stronger than the other,
Or the two
Will merge, then I'm another.
Perhaps one day
I'll find the real 'I',
But until then,
One will laugh
And the other will cry.

February 1991

Days of Innocence,
Days of laughter,
Days of learning and
Days of growth.

Spring meant renewal,
Summer brought sunshine and
Autumn would glow,
Before white Winter snow.

Memories of yesterday,
Days of childhood,
Long ago.

February 1991

Rekindled memories after a tree was planted in Matthew's memory in the grounds of the village school

The miracle of Spring seems a mockery,
Rubbing salt into the wound.
New life in triumph rises from the earth
But not my son.
In despair I close my eyes to the wonder of rebirth.

March 1991

Now comes indeed, the end of all delight,
  The end of forward-looking on life's way,
  The end of all desire to pierce the night
For gleam of hope, the end of all things gay;
The end to any promise Spring might hold,
The end of praying and, O God, the end
Of love that waited to be shared and told;
Now evermore shall life with sorrow blend.

Part of *To Billy, My Son* by Vera Bax
for her son killed in action, May 15th 1945

She was an elderly lady
  With soft expression
  And cotton wool hair.
Compassion shone from her blue eyes
And her gentle voice conveyed understanding.
God had given her a special gift.
She used her gift to help me
Giving proof of what I'd always felt —
Life does not end with death.

March 1991

I wish, my son, you had not gone.
I wish, my son, you'd stayed at home.
I wish, my son, you'd been asleep
  but the night was dark
  and you had a rendezvous to keep.

You were adventurous but cautious.
You would always weigh the pros and cons,
prepare well before the daring leap
  but the night was dark
  and you had a rendezvous to keep.

I'm glad you lived your life to the full,
with ambitions and dreams uniquely your own
and that your feelings were real and honest and deep
  on that night so dark
  when you had a rendezvous to keep.

How I love you, my son, for all that you were
How I love you, my son, for all you'd have been.
Nothing consoles, I shall forever weep
  when I remember that night so dark,
  when you had a rendezvous to keep.

I wish, my son, we had not gone.
I wish, my son, we'd been with you
to hold you close through your last sleep,
  on that night so dark
  when you had a rendezvous to keep.
  Alone.

March 1991

I read a poem written by B D Van Vechten following the death of his son
— it stayed with me in part, especially the lines *but the night was dark
and you had a rendezvous to keep*. It seemed so fitting that I wrote this,
much of which is probably similar to Ben Van Vechten's composition, in
his book *The First Year of Forever*.

When grief was permanently stable
it was somehow more safe to live with.
Because it was so obviously there
it didn't catch me, or others, unaware.
I knew when and how it would expose itself through me
and was prepared for the emotions it would force me
to face.
But though grief is woven indelibly into my being,
it is less consistent now.
It sometimes retreats,
relieved to escape the limelight for awhile,
lulling me into false security;
then confused, it rushes back again
with powerful vengeance,
protesting at its dismissal
and, almost despite itself,
it burdens me with pain anew
letting me know its need for recognition
as yet another raw nerve is discovered and exposed.

April 1991

Perhaps

Perhaps one day the sun will shine again
And I shall see that still the skies are blue,
And feel once more I do not live in vain
Although bereft of you.

Perhaps the golden meadows at my feet
Will make the sunny hours of Spring seem gay,
And I shall find the white May blossom sweet
Though you have passed away.

Perhaps the Summer woods will shimmer bright
And crimson roses once again be fair,
and Autumn harvest fields a rich delight
Although you are not there.

Perhaps some day I shall not shrink in pain,
To see the passing of the dying year
And listen to the Christmas songs again
Although you cannot hear.

But though kind time may many joys renew
There is one greatest joy I shall not know
Again, because my heart, for loss of you
was broken, long ago.

Anon

I was very touched to be given this poem by Claire, a friend's daughter, who came across it at school and copied it for me.

I've been watching the Iris
   gracefully growing,
   so serene,
slender body
delicate sheen,
protective leaves,
deeper green.

Slowly bud unfolds to flower
veined petals
deepest blue,
blending with
a softer hue
reminding me
so much of you.

The beauty of your soulful eyes,
the sun-loving Iris vivifies.

May 1991

During the night
   one of grief's accomplices,
   the one who stole my senses,
returned to give them back
and today, with mixed feelings,
I felt something stirring within.

The honeysuckle grabbed my attention
as I breathed its heady scent
and I held the blue Iris without crumbling,
admiring its graceful form.

Rejoicing in the sound,
I heard birds sing
and bees hum
and Concorde overhead.

The warmth of the sun caressed me
and the springy grass beneath my feet
put a bounce into my step;
and I laughed a proper laugh.

Tonight I cried,
feeling confused and guilty,
not knowing how to deal
with 'normality' creeping back.

Half-mended threads of life
dangle before me;
are they strong enough to hold me?
Or I to hold them?
If they, or I, should break
it will be I who falls.
I don't know if I am scared
to pick them up again,
or if I just don't want to.

May 1991

*You joked, and now are silent, down the years
your wit shall be remembered and revived.
For this blind instant suffer us our tears —
you always drew our laughter while you lived.*

After Alamein by Prudence Macdonald

The Second Year

June will never again be warm,
It will always be a month of storm,
No matter how bright the sun.

No matter how radiant the rose,
My heart with sorrow knows,
June will evermore be dull.

June, a month that used to be so gay,
Now has death stamped on a day,
And it cannot be erased.

No, nothing can erase the pain,
For June will come again and again,
But Matthew never will.

June 1991

We miss your smile and the times of sharing;
The chats, the jokes, the teasing, the caring.
We miss your laughter and your zest for
living;
Your gentle side and your joy in giving.
Your sunny nature so warm and true,
Reflects in our beautiful memories of you.

14th June 1991
on Matt's first anniversary

For so long I had wanted to know,
but never expected to know —
Knowing hasn't eased the pain.
Could I ever have really have thought it might?

But I'm grateful to know,
to be given this opportunity
to see things more clearly -
But my vision is blurred just now.

I wasn't shocked by the explanation.
I felt I already knew
but wanted confirmation,
an explanation which made sense —
It does, a cruel sense.

And the questions still mount.

How long was it there,
that bloody time-bomb
ticking away to count-down?
Lurking, hideously waiting
for the planned moment to explode,
as it did, without warning,
the shock causing an end to Matt's life
and shattering ours.

I was told
"If not then it would have been soon".
Was the mechanism faulty?
Was the timer wrong?
Was then the 'right' time?
No. No time is the 'right' time to die
for one on the threshold of life;
nor for us, left grieving.

We cannot make sense of it yet, if ever,
and as for you Matthew,
what about for you?
Deep in your soul did you know?
Is that why every minute had to be filled?
Was your life span accomplished according to God's
    plan?
Did you need only eighteen years
of this earthly school?
Were you that advanced in your evolution
or has it all been a terrible mistake?

And so it goes on,
a wheel ever turning.
So many questions
relentlessly crowding my mind;
so many ponderables, so many answers
each creating yet another question.

August 1991

Do not stand at my grave and weep
I am not there, I do not sleep.

I am a thousand winds that blow,
I am the diamond glints on snow,
I am the sunlight on ripened grain,
I am the gentle autumn rain.

When you awaken in the morning hush,
I am the uplifting rush
Of quiet birds in circled flight,
I am the soft stars that shine at night.

Do not stand at my grave and cry,
I am not there, I did not die.

These lines are believed to be
the burial prayer of the Makah
tribe of North American Indians

I hide my grief throughout the weary days,
  And gather up the threads of life again,
  Now, when I feel my courage flicker low,
Your spirit comes to breathe it into flame,
Until I lift my head, and smiling go,
Whispering softly your beloved name.

And yet to me it seems but yesterday
You were a child, and full of childish fears:
Then I would run to you and soothe away
The loneliness of night, and dry your tears;
But now you are the comforter, and keep,
From out the shadows, watch, lest I should weep.

From *To Richard My Son* by Vera Bax
Richard was killed in action on 17th August 1942

Here in our hearts
  Love lives forever,
  Dying never,
Physically apart,
Spiritually together.

8th October 1991
Matthew's 20th birthday

65

They say you will not come again,
but I shall always hear your voice
in silence and in song, and feel you ever
near.

They say that you have passed beyond,
unto the joy supreme, but I can always
call you back into the land of dream.

For death is but a gateway to the great
reality, a new beginning,
not an end to human destiny.

Love is all, and life goes on in spite
of grief and pain, and deep within my heart
I know that we shall meet again.

Anon

The first Christmas without Matt
I seemed to grope through in a blur.
I can remember the pain, the panic,
the despair, the disbelief,
the desperate longing
and the feeling of futility.
I was a clockwork toy,
with an invisible hand turning the key.
And yet somehow I coped.
Little did I know I was being protected
by a kind and weary mind;
shielded, cushioned by a semi-numbness.
In zombie fashion I survived it,
later only remembering it through a mental fog.
But now my once protective mind,
battling against redundancy,
is urging me to reality
and I am more aware.
I am scared.
Scared of the emotions welling inside me.
Terrified that this time I won't cope,
that the flimsy thread of sanity will snap;
that the strength I can so often muster
will desert me;
that I won't be able to bear the strain of pretence
and hopelessness will overwhelm me.
I'll give up.
I already feel I'm on the verge of crumbling.
It would be so much easier to hibernate   *(continues)*

into a world of my own,
not emerging until it's over.

Anniversaries, birthdays, though just as painful,
just as sad,
just as devastating
are more personal:
the world doesn't celebrate whilst I grieve.
But Christmas,
Christmas involves everyone.
Jollity all around,
I can't escape it,
the streets, the shops, immersed in torturing gaiety.
Matthew revelled in it,
the excitement, the shopping, the parties and
  celebrations;
a favourite time of the year for him,
rivalling the heat of summer.

A favourite time of the year for him . . .

Wild scribbling, now suddenly I'm calm,
strength replacing fearful weakness
and Matthew fixed firmly in my mind.
I can almost hear him say
"It's a challenge, Mum. Go for it."
And so I will.
I'll give it my best.

late November 1991

68

If I should die and leave you here awhile,
Be not like others, sore undone, who keep
Lone vigils by the silent dust and weep . . .

For my sake, turn again to life and smile,
Nerving thy heart and trembling hand to do
Something to comfort weaker hearts than thine . . .

Complete these dear, unfinished tasks of mine,
And I, perchance, may therein comfort you . . .

from *A Warrior on Wings*

I was looking for a library book for my mother-in-law one day, when a strange thing happened. A book fell off the shelf; I picked it up and it opened at the page with this poem. I copied it right away — it seemed like a message.

Returning home from midnight Mass,
I lit a candle just for you,
Knowing you'd be close to us
And you would see it too.

I talked to you of Christmasses past
And of things you used to do,
Recalling how our gifts we'd hide,
No place was safe from you!

I told you how I longed for you,
Not dwelling on the pain,
I didn't want to make you sad,
Only to explain.

(continues)

Yet I couldn't promise not to cry,
For crying brings relief,
Nor could I promise not to mourn,
Or put aside my grief.

But I promised I would always live
A part of each day for you;
And I would try to do those things
You'd be proud for me to do.

I wished you peace and sent you love,
Then I said "Goodnight",
Asking God to care for you
And guide you by His light.

early hours of Christmas morning, 1991

*I*n this sad world of ours, sorrow comes to all.
It comes with bitterest agony.
Perfect relief is not possible, except with time.
You cannot now realise that you will ever feel better.

And yet this is a mistake.
You are sure to be happy again.
To know this, which is certainly true,
Will make you less miserable now.

I have experienced enough to know what I say.

by Abraham Lincoln (who lost three sons)

from *Helping each other through the seasons of grief*, published by The Compassionate Friends

Safety precautions taken,
    we had braved ourselves for the climb.
    Gingerly we gained ground
avoiding the obvious dangers,
ever wary of the invisible crevices
so easy to fall into.

With tentative steps
we wearily advanced,
fighting an army of emotions,
controlling our actions,
controlling our voices,
aware that battle fatigue could lead to errors,
knowing one wrong move, one fearful cry
could cause an avalanche
of suffocating pain and darkness,
knowing one onslaught could trigger another
and another
and rescue would be difficult.

Though we struggled and often stumbled
we made it.
With heavy packs
and feet that slid on icy ground
we fought our way,
another mountain climbed;
albeit with a sense of relief
rather than with a sense of victory,
for we are reluctant conquerors
not welcoming the feelings of resignation
now frozen in our minds.

January 1992

Today, in the churchyard, I spied snowdrops,
shyly peeping above the frosty grass.
A wintry sun, affording them some warmth,
received gentle nods of contented approval.
So tiny, so delicate,
yet they had braved the winter
in the dark,
out of sight
until, obeying nature's law
they rose again
into the light.

And Matthew, like the snowdrop,
has left the darkness behind;
his soul has taken flight,
in harmony with God's law,
eternally growing
in His light.

January 1992

I slept in the spare room last night.
Settling with a book
I was aware of eyes on me,
and looking upward
saw Bunny and the other soft toys
peering down from the wardrobe top.
That's all it took, his look
and the pain beneath the surface
rose and overwhelmed.

I never read,
Bunny shared my bed
and my anguish.
How I wished he could speak,
he'd have had so much to tell,
this well-worn and much-loved friend.

Matthew's confidant and comforter
from childhood days,
last night was mine.

February, 1992

73

Raindrops, drop after drop,
slide down the window
like the tears on my cheeks.
Outside, naked trees shiver
in the gusty wind.
The bird-bath, brimming with water
remains empty.
No living creature stirs, except
from time to time
a crow will venture
towards the grey and charcoal clouds,
racing with them
across a mournful sky.
Puddles dancing with circular movement
form on the patio.
The bench at the bottom of the garden
stands forlorn,
in summer I sense you there
but not today.
All is silent
save for the patter of the rain
and the clock behind me
ticking to the sound of your name.

February, 1992

The sun, filtering through your blind,
throws a vivid striped pattern
across your bed,
leaving your pillow in shadow.
Beyond your window,
trees framed by a cool blue sky,
sway in the busy breeze
which now and then urges
the tall, blue-green pine,
to peep into your room.

Here there is divine peace.
The quietness and stillness,
so hard at first
to come to terms with,
somehow speaks of you.
So much of you is here
in the silence.
I feel you in my heartbeat
and two souls touch.

It's here I come, to write, to think
and I never feel alone,
your warmth enfolds me.
Though out of sight
I know you are not lost to me,
you will always be a part of me
and I of you,
my spirit son.

February 1992

Your tree in the churchyard, though just a sapling,
is already preparing for a Spring-time display.
Reddish-brown twig-like branches
fan their way skyward,
proudly showing their tiny secretive buds.
Through the grass around the slim trunk,
cream coloured crocus, mindful of later competition
bloom now, seeking from us deserved admiration,
joyous celebration of God's gift of re-birth.

February 1992

Rescued daffodils,
victims of last night's wind,
bring Spring into your room.
Warm, bright, full of promise
yellow sings to me of you.
Your room is filled with you,
with sunshine
and I am pleased.
Last year sunshine made me cry.

Eyes drawn to your prided yellow baseball cap
I manage a salty smile,
remembering how you made us laugh
and how you laughed with us,
last time you wore it.
Your quick wit and quiet humour
will never be forgotten,
it will always light my memory —
'The Sunshine Kid' you'll always be.

March 1992

76

A mild March breeze awakens Springtime buds.
Yellow in abundance colours my walk
and eagerly I accept its welcome upliftment.
Lush shiny celandines
nestle in the shelter of hedgerows and ditches,
making dull places bright,
whilst friendly crocus open wide in invitation
to a teasing lemon sun.
Along the roadside and in field and wood,
pale tranquil primroses grace their chosen places
with a serenity which adds calm to this busy season.
Over the vicarage wall
forsythia, waiting with mixed anticipation,
sneaks a peep at the daffodils still in bud,
knowing their splendour will soon detract from hers.

In the churchyard,
an advanced array of these Springtime messengers
weaves a myriad of sunshine hues through the grass
and over loved ones' graves.
Holding aloft their golden trumpets they sway,
as they play to the rhythm of the wind,
music orchestrated by The Great Composer,
strains too mystical for human ears.
All before me personifies a caring God.
Each unfolding bud speaks of continuity,
a veiled view of heaven's promise.

(continues)

I thought all promise gone,
that you had taken all your sunshine with you
but I was wrong;
for today Matt, with eyes not wholly mine,
I see in the glory all around
just how much you've left behind.

March 1992

Steps and walking,
Looking and seeing,
Feeling and knowing
That Matthew was here.

Listening and touching,
Stirring within,
All the days of your life
Will always begin —
With Matthew.

Gone but not gone,
Just out of reach
For I know he is close,
And always will be,
Matthew your son,
His spirit set free.

by Maureen (mother of Claire, *Perhaps*, page 57), March 1992

We had been talking about Matthew a short time before Maureen wrote this. She said she picked up a pencil and without even thinking, the words just flowed.

I knelt before Her with open heart,
childhood faith re-kindled.
The crowds melted into the vastness,
obscured by the growing flame of my candle.
Notre Dame became hushed and still,
voices borne away on a wisp of smoke.

Bathed in the glow of fervent petitions
we seemed alone,
just Her and I.
Her eyes, no longer painted stone,
gazed gently, deeply into mine.
Her love and compassion filled me
and I knew she had heard my prayer.
She understood, for she too
had felt a sword of sorrow pierce her heart.
She absorbed my tears, uplifted me.
Her warmth and peace enfolded me
and something else —
the nearness of you
and the awareness you instil
that all is well.

I embraced the moment;
holding it, storing it, breathing it in
until, with earthly senses returning,
the smell of wax and stone and polished wood
invaded my nostrils.
Voices and people drifted back
and far too soon all became as it was before,
except me. *(continues)*

Through the shimmering quivering haze
I could have sworn I saw Her smile.
Or was it just the flickering candles
encouraging movement to play around her face?

May 1992

I felt you walk
  unseen, unheard, beside us
  through the gardens of Giverny,
delighting in the scented colours
of Monet's Springtime palette.

Such joyful inspiration,
contrasting, blending,
in thoughtful creativity,
designed without rigidity
in the artist's fertile mind.

Too soon for poppies,
but did you see
the iris and azalea, the lilac
and blossoms on the bough?

Did you too, catch your breath,
at the beauty of the canvas
stretched before the house?
Clouds of pink tulips
floating above a sea
of deep blue forget-me-nots.

Did you stop awhile
beneath the wisteria
on the Japanese bridge,
soaking up the soft reflection
of weeping willow and clear blue sky,
wishing the water-lilies would flower early
to complete the unfinished picture?
Were you aware of my contentment,
aware that I felt you there
in the mystical magic of the place,
on every pathway,
in every view?

And in the house I sensed you,
the smell of polish luring you
and the furniture and the canvasses
and the Japanese prints.

And in the studio
when, under heightened sensitivity,
I started to crumble,
I felt your support,
felt you urging me
not to mar the wonder of the day.
I felt your strength and your peace
and your need to feel mine.

May, 1992

Beautiful May morn.
Birds in splendid chorus
usher in the dawn.
Pale daybreak,
laced with golden hue,
sweet promise of sunshine,
sweet memories of you.

May 1992

Mid-day in the garden.
Sitting in the sun
I watch a blackbird bathing,
oblivious to the heat
his friends seek shelter from.
Tucked in trees and bushes they hide,
their presence made known
by chirping and chattering
and squawks from families arguing
in overcrowded nests.
In the distance
the cuckoo, relieved of responsibility,
boasts her artfulness
for everyone to hear.

The flower beds are alive with colour
and the sound of velvet bees.
A white butterfly
gracefully manoeuvres between the blooms,
resting for a moment
on the cerise azalea;
the one you bought for Fathers' Day,
the year before you went away.

I close my eyes
and in snapshot fashion
scenes appear of
paddling pool, pets,
swings and games,   *(continues)*

of tents and torchlight
and feasts at midnight,
of gardening, sunbathing
and
a portable telly under an umbrella,
Wimbledon in the sun.

Gentle memories, tinged with sadness,
prompt the tears to flow,
yet I know
things have improved.
You are still always on my mind
but I recall your life now
more often that your passing.

I open my eyes
sensing your presence.
The bench at the bottom of the garden
does not remain empty today.

May 1992

O Matt, I miss you so.
　　　The grin, the walk,
　　　The cosy talk,
The smile as you waved
'Goodbye'.
Your music and singing,
The 'phone always ringing,
The hectic weekends,
Your untidy room.

I miss snacks at midnight,
Lunch in the sunlight
And your delight at
Toad-in-the-hole.
The grapefruit shared,
The way you cared;
Your hope, your joy
Of each day.
And the winning wink.

I miss sharing with you
So many,
Ordinary, everyday things,
We'd put the world right,
Hot chocolate at night.
I miss sharing secrets
And jokes,
And how you muddled
The months.　　　　　　　　　　　　*(continues)*

I miss all of your clutter
And all of your mess,
Your laid-backness,
Your determinedness
And arguments
And discussions
And your searching mind,
So full of 'Why's?'.
And your gifted eyes
And gifted hands.
Your keen sense of smell.

I miss the diverseness
Of you.
Your strength
And your gentleness.
Joy in a flower,
Weight-lifting power
And after a shower,
Draped in a towel,
Hair fixed with Gel.
Always late.

I miss caring for you
And waiting for you
To arrive with a
Cheerful "Hi".
I miss laughing with you
And shouting at you

And fussing to
Straighten your tie.
And warming your feet.

I miss the piles of washing,
Clothes on the floor
And so much more.
The hassle of waking you up;
How you'd rush for
The papers,
Never missing your stars,
Yours often true
— O, how I miss you.

I miss the way
You cracked your fingers,
Picked your toes,
Wrinkled your nose,
Faces you made.
You made me laugh,
You were a clown.
You were my friend.
I never thought
It would end.
O Matt, I miss you so.

May 1992

Into the Third Year

May has gone,
　　　its last fine day
　　　has given way
To June so grey.

Grey air, grey clouds
and grey, grey rain,
grey thoughts run riot
through my brain
where melancholy, creeping back
invades the grey to turn it black.

O June, I feel you prise apart
the unhealed scar, the broken heart.

June 1992

We talked of Aberfan from time to time before ..
but we never visited.
Somehow it seemed wrong
but not now
for we were visiting with empathy
and some understanding
and not just sympathetic curiosity.
We felt somehow we had been granted permission,
yet we approached with apprehension,
not wanting to offend.

The graves on the hillside
beckoned beneath gracious arches,
leading the eye beyond
to a promise of an invisible heaven.

John managed to read a few headstones,
but the enormity of it all overwhelmed him.
Our grief and the grief of others weighed upon him
and silently weeping, he slowly moved on.

Pausing at each grave
my heart soaked up the sorrow of the words
as a sponge,
wringing out its heaviness in tears,
my 'why?' permeating the tranquillity,
disturbing those dormant whys
hanging unanswered in the air all around.

I prayed those other seekers,
though not privy to the whole plan,
have, like us,
been allowed a glimpse.
I have faith enough to know
the children are safe,
sadly missed and always longed for
but safe and free from earthly strife;
but my heart goes out to those left behind
with scars that will never truly heal.

In the village,
where the brave bereaved who still survive
have gathered up the threads of life again,
I perceived 'normality' in the shadow of disaster,
making its presence known;
but the reality of the magnitude
of suffering and loss
filled me with sadness and unforgettable awe.

June 1992

8.30pm. It was a mistake to go.
I should have known better
but I wanted to leave flowers
at the roadside,
we'd managed it last year,
the first year,
finding the place easily;
the tree still bore the scars
and broken branches
and it still loomed large
and menacing
and capable of destruction.

Tonight the trees appeared smaller,
insignificant and similar,
no obvious damage apparent,
no distinguishing criminal marks;
and the ditch I remembered
as being far from the road,
in reality is only a few paces
but just as dark and foreboding
though disguised beneath an abundance
of dense, living cover.
Nature had worked against us,
or maybe for us,
burying all evidence
of the devastation caused,
making it impossible
to find the exact place.

With mounting panic and distress
we left our flowers
where our instincts guided us,
eager to be away.
Last year I sensed you with us
but not this year, two years on.
You want us to forget this place.
Dad was right.
Next year I'll know better.

June 13th, the eve of Matt's second anniversary

You'll be with us always
in the years that lie ahead.
When miracles of Spring abound,
we'll hear your voice in nature's sound
and feel your joy when poppies red,
through the meadows gaily spread.
In the years that lie ahead
you'll be with us always.

You'll be with us always
in the years that lie ahead.
When June arrives with pain each year
we know we'll feel your presence near
and when the days are filled with dread,
love will flow when tears are shed.
In the years that lie ahead
you'll be with us always.

You'll be with us always
in the years that lie ahead.
When trees for your birthday put on a show
of rich mellow colours, Autumn's warm glow,
we're sure that you'll see with eyes far from dead,
for you do not sleep in that green grassy bed.
In the years that lie ahead
you'll be with us always.

You'll be with us always
in the years that lie ahead.
Through each Winter of our grief
fond memories will bring relief
and your love of life will fill each head,
though Christmas wreaths adorn death's bed.
In the years that lie ahead
you'll be with us always.

June 1992

I thought I'd never again be whole;
that the legacy of loss,
that immeasurable void within
where longing dwells,
would render me forever incomplete;
but now I find that the emptiness
is filling with you.
You grow in the space
as a child in the womb.
Roles reversed, you nurture me
and wholeness seems a possibility —
Perhaps?

June 1992

Gentle day, soft sky,
   Soft clouds, soft sigh.

Sweet air, soft rain,
Soft sorrow, soft pain.

Dancing leaves, soft sound,
Soft music, soft ground.

Quiet whisper, soft breeze,
Soft heart, soft squeeze.

Hazy sun, soft light,
Soft shadows, soft sight.

Pastel rainbow, soft hue,
Soft memories, soft you.

Soft stillness, thoughts cease,
God's love, soft peace.

July 1992

You are there in the dance of creation,
In the rhythm of sea and of sky,
In the music of wind and of water,
In the seasons of life passing by.

You are there attuned to the wonder
Of nature's perpetual art,
In beauty, in song and in laughter,
A bow for the strings of my heart.

In space and time you are woven,
Through memories you entwine,
Continuous thread in His pattern,
Eternal in His design.

July 1992

Something tugged at my heartstrings today
as I watched the washing billow on the line.
It's been awhile now since the missing clothes
were all I saw in my mind's eye,
the impact of their absence immense.
You produced more washing than the rest of us
put together.

I've almost grown accustomed
to only washing for three
and shopping for three
and cooking for three;
though sometimes I am caught unawares
and will set the table for four,
having to remove cutlery and mat
with shaking hands and heavy heart.

The scent of softener drifts on the air.
You liked the smell —
but not on football gear or PE kit!
I remember how you loved freshly laundered sheets
and towels
and how you 'helped' me iron hankies
when you were small,
neatly folding them.
You were tidy then.

The breeze caresses the washing dry.
A tear is gently brushed from my eye.
The breeze? Or an unseen hand?

August 1992

We gather, celebrations to share,
With Granny and Grand-dad,
The Golden pair.
Kisses, hugs, warm embrace,
Family, friends,
Missing face.

Speech from Dad,
Courageous host.
Glasses raised
We drink a toast
And through the smiles
And the happy cheer
We wish, how we wish,
That you were here.

"But I am, in spirit,"
A voice seems to say,
"Looking in for a while
on this special day."

Cake is cut,
We feel the strain,
We swallow hard,
The searing pain.

Music, songs from bygone years,
Laughter, gossip,
Hidden tears.

August 1992

Spring and Winter,
    Beginnings, ends,
    Parents, children,
Lovers, friends —
All will pass.

Summer, Autumn,
Sun and rain,
Sorrow, joy,
Seasoned pain —
All will pass.

Storm and calm,
Shade and light,
Darkest day,
Bleakest night —
All will pass.

Deafness hear,
Darkness see,
Jailed released,
Captive free —
All will pass.

Birth and death,
Body, soul,
Spirit soaring
To its goal —
All will pass.

All will pass
And yet remain,
Loving link,
Unbroken chain.

August 1992

I will not bind you to me
In sorrow and despair,
I could not be that selfish
In cruelty unfair.
No emotional blackmail
I know that's not for me,
I miss you to distraction
But I want you to be free.

Love, wisdom, peace;
These I wish you
In your eternal life
And I wish for your fulfilment,
Not bound by earthly strife.

For I know as you journey onward,
We will never be truly apart,
For my love travels with you
And your love lives in my heart.

September 1992

The tempo is changing, slowing down.
   The vitality of summer sinks ever further
   into the dying year,
her glory drowned and battered by ceaseless rain;
her heady scents smothered
by November smells of fermentation and decay;
yet it's still September.
It seems as though the seasons,
like me, have lost their sense of time.

But the sun shone yesterday
showing a more familiar autumn.
Behind the damp curtain
Mother Nature had waved her wand,
casting another seasonal spell,
turning green to red and gold and rust,
marking the way for October's advance.

I want October to be beautiful,
bright with life,
as it was on the day you were born;
when sun, filtering through the early morning mist,
touched the frost and made it sparkle
and touched the bushes,
adorning them with diamond-studded lace.
Colour sang and rustled amidst the glowing leaves
and love gave birth
in the warmth and stillness of the day.

I want peace to permeate the sadness of your 21st.
I want to feel gladness for the life you had,
not bitterness for all that's been denied.
I want to think of you, with delight over-riding sorrow
and be thankful for the joy of knowing you,
of loving you,
of loving you still.
I'll always feel pride at the mention of your name.
I want to hear your name, speak your name
and feel at peace.

September 1992

I can remember times when, paralysed with pain,
I hoped madness might release me,
then feared it would
and clung to the pain
and called it love.

Time passed and this painful love
became an aching love, awash with sorrow
and the true love, hidden, but always there,
began to suffocate in the confusion of its burden,
wanting only to be love alone.

I can remember the despair of this aching love,
trapped within my grief
and how I struggled to free it,
to give it back its joy.

For joy you were, a precious gift,
bright gem without a flaw.
And the joy of you
will for evermore remain,
uplifting love, to soften pain,
urging hope to rise again.

October 1992

Your 21st has gone.
    The toast I'd planned
    was swallowed, without cheer
and now I face the beginning
of the end,
of another dying year,
with its fearful, tearful, festive days
that carol through bleak barrenness;
to echo in my hollowness.

During Summer
I gave thought to Winter,
message read with heart not eye,
saw the reason for the season,
for all to live first have to die.
But now; sweet melancholy,
soft as shadows,
falls around your absence
and your name;
and though I know
'hope springs eternal'
life will never be the same,
for seasons rise, before our eyes,
but not so you.

(continues)

So tears of longing, long will flow,
for the loveliness I will not know,
as time and reality,
side by side,
force my mind to open wide,
to all the joys I've been denied.
For never will I hug
with earthly pride,
the man I knew you'd grow to be,
nor kiss your children,
tell them stories;
hold them, lovingly close to me.

October 1992

Remembering that age too seldom gives
What youth has dreamed; our hopes are
mostly vain
And fortunate indeed is he who lives
Forever young, beyond the pain.

from *The Fallen* by Vera Bax

About the author

Ann and John have lived near Newbury, in Berkshire, since 1971.

Ann had not planned to return to work until the boys were in secondary education, but shortly after Matthew joined Daniel at the village primary school, she was offered a post assisting the infant teacher. She stayed there for ten years, later returning to secretarial work.

At the time of Matthew's accident, she was employed as a receptionist for a firm of fine art auctioneers. Now, however, she has completely changed direction, deriving much pleasure and satisfaction working part-time as a carer in a nursing home, and doing a little voluntary work.

Ann is convinced that the 'scribbling' she began gradually became a form of therapy for her. That — together with the sad yet comforting awareness through The Compassionate Friends that she was not alone in her grief — helped her retain her sanity.

Ann is sharing the royalties on this volume of poems between The Compassionate Friends, and Helen House (the first children's hospice). Both organisations express their deep appreciation of this thoughtful gesture.

The Compassionate Friends
53 North Street
Bristol BS3 1EN
☎ 0272 539 639

Helen House
37 Leopold St
Oxford OX4 1QT
☎ 0865 728 251

Acknowledgements

The poems on pages 15, 24, 50, 54, 59, 65 and 107 all come from the book *Chaos of the Night*, selected and edited by Catherine W Reilly, published by Virago Press, 1984. Their assistance in obtaining permission to include the poems here is gratefully acknowledged.

page

15   Marion Coleman: 'Monte Cassino 1945' from *Myself Is All I Have*, Outposts Publications, 1969

24   Patricia M Saunders: '20th Century Requiem' from *Arena*, Hutchinson & Co, 1948

50   Barbara Catherine Edwards: 'Bomb Incident' from *Poems from Hospital*, Outposts Publications, 1962

54   Vera Bax: 'To Billy, My Son' previously unpublished

59   Prudence Macdonald: 'After Alamein' from *No Wasted Hour*, Sidgwick & Jackson, 1945

65   Vera Bax: 'To Richard, My Son', *Distaff Muse* (ed Bax and Stewart), Hollis & Carter, 1949

107   Vera Bax: 'The Fallen' from *Anthology for Verse Speakers* (ed Pertwee), Samuel French, 1950. Reprinted by permission of Mrs Bax's Literary Executor

54   B D Van Vechten: *The First Year of Forever*, Dwight Publishing (Ohio, USA), 1982

34, 70 *Helping each other through the seasons of grief* is published by The Compassionate Friends (53 North Street, Bristol BS3 1EN, £3 incl p&p)

If permission has inadvertently been omitted, please write to Arthur James Limited (One Cranbourne Road, London N10 2BT, England) with the relevant information and this will be included in the next edition.